Visual Geography Series®

UNITED STATES

...in Pictures

Prepared by
Geography Department

Lerner Publications Company
Minneapolis

Independent Picture Service

**An angler nets a trout from a stream in Colorado, a
western state of mountains and plains.**

This book is an all-new edition in the Visual Geography Series. Previous editions were published by
Sterling Publishing Company, New York City. The
text, set in 10/12 Century Textbook, is fully revised
and updated, and new photographs, maps, charts, and
captions have been added.

LIBRARY OF CONGRESS CATALOGING-IN-PUBLICATION DATA

> **United States in pictures** / prepared by Geography Dept.,
> Lerner Publications Co.
>   p.   cm. — (Visual geography series)
>   Includes index.
>   ISBN 0-8225-1896-1 (lib. bdg.)
>   1. United States—Geography. 2. United States—
> Pictorial works. [1. United States.] I. Lerner Publica-
> tions Company. Geography Dept. II. Series: Visual
> geography series (Minneapolis, Minn.)
> E161.3.U72 1995
> 917.3—dc20   94-44841
>   CIP
>   AC

International Standard Book Number: 0-8225-1896-1
Library of Congress Catalog Card Number: 94-44841

VISUAL GEOGRAPHY SERIES®

Publisher
Harry Jonas Lerner
Senior Editor
Mary M. Rodgers
Editors
Tom Streissguth
Colleen Sexton
Photo Researcher
Cindy Hartmon
Editorial/Photo Assistant
Marybeth Campbell
Consultants/Contributors
Karen Sirvaitis
Sandra K. Davis
Designer
Jim Simondet
Cartographer
Carol F. Barrett
Indexer
Sylvia Timian
Production Manager
Gary J. Hansen

Courtesy of Utah Travel Council

**A Native American rancher lets his animals graze on a
Navajo reservation in Utah.**

Acknowledgments

Title page photo by Roger Bickel/New England
Stock Photo.

Elevation contours adapted from *The Times Atlas of
the World*, seventh comprehensive edition (New
York: Times Books, 1985).

1 2 3 4 5 6 – JR – 00 99 98 97 96 95

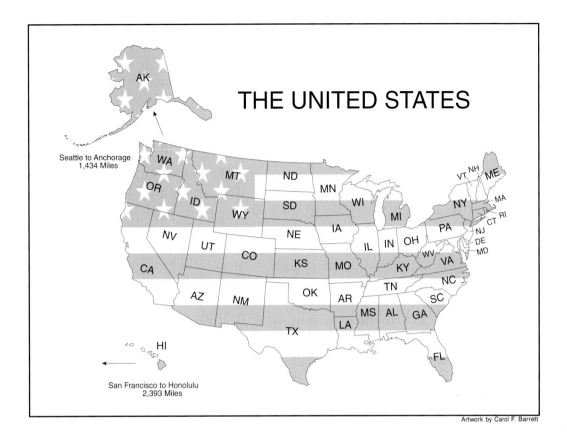

Seattle to Anchorage
1,434 Miles

THE UNITED STATES

San Francisco to Honolulu
2,393 Miles

Artwork by Carol F. Barrett

Contents

CANADA

Seattle
Portland
Columbia R.
Grand Coulee
Dam
Snake R.
YELLOWSTONE
NAT. PK.
GRAND TETON
NAT. PK.
MT. RUSHMORE
NAT. MEM.
Reno
Sacramento
San
Jose
YOSEMITE
NAT. PK.
BRYCE CANYON
NAT. PK.
Hoover
Dam
Colorado R.
CANYONLANDS
NAT. PK.
Los
Angeles
San
Diego
GRAND CANYON
NAT. PK.
CHACO CULTURE
NAT. HIST. PK.
Gila R.

PACIFIC
OCEAN

THE
GREAT LAKES
L. Superior
L. Michigan
Huron
L. Ontario
L. Erie
St. Lawrence Seaway
Saratoga
Newport
Boston
Plymouth
MARTHA'S
VINEYARD
Madison
Missouri R.
Chicago
New York
Philadelphia
Baltimore
Dover
WASHINGTON
D.C.
Chesapeake Bay
St. Louis
Ohio R.
Potomac R.
Yorktown
Jamestown
(Ruins)
Mississippi R.
Tennessee R.

Fort Worth

Houston

New
Orleans

Atlanta

St. Augustine
Orlando

ATLANTIC
OCEAN

Gulf of
California

MEXICO

Gulf of Mexico

Key West

Point Barrow

DENALI NAT. PK.

CANADA

State Boundaries

Major Roads

0   250   500 Miles
0   250   500 Kilometers

PACIFIC OCEAN

Honolulu

Kawaihae

0   100   200 Miles
0   100   200 Kilometers

HAWAII I.

ARCTIC
OCEAN

60°
50°
70°
160°
30°
PACIFIC
OCEAN

ATLANTIC
OCEAN

20°

NORTH AMERICA
UNITED STATES

0   1000 Miles
0   1000 Kilometers

METRIC CONVERSION CHART
To Find Approximate Equivalents

WHEN YOU KNOW:	MULTIPLY BY:	TO FIND:
AREA		
acres	0.41	hectares
square miles	2.59	square kilometers
CAPACITY		
gallons	3.79	liters
LENGTH		
feet	30.48	centimeters
yards	0.91	meters
miles	1.61	kilometers
MASS (weight)		
pounds	0.45	kilograms
tons	0.91	metric tons
VOLUME		
cubic yards	0.77	cubic meters
TEMPERATURE		
degrees Fahrenheit	0.56 (*after* subtracting 32)	degrees Celsius

More than 90 percent of the land in Iowa is devoted to farming, with corn, soybeans, hay, oats, and alfalfa being the primary crops. The fertile soil of this midwestern state drew settlers from the eastern United States in the 1800s.

Introduction

The United States of America spans central North America from the Atlantic to the Pacific oceans. From its small beginnings in settlements along the Atlantic coast, the United States has grown into one of the largest and richest nations on earth.

The country's size and varied natural resources have not only contributed to its wealth but also have attracted millions of immigrants. In the 1800s, the nation's eastern urban areas swelled as people came to work in growing factories. Mean-while, the prospect of owning land or finding gold drew many thousands to the plains and mountains far to the west.

The United States developed into the world's leading agricultural nation, raising enough food not only to feed its own population but also for export. The industrial variety of the United States—ranging from the production of cars to the manufacturing of computers—puts the country in economic competition with the rest of the world. The nation's political clout, which developed slowly, is now felt on every continent. Involvement in foreign affairs and the breakup of the Soviet Union have turned the United States into the world's only superpower.

Compared to most other nations, the United States is militarily, politically, and economically strong. Yet domestic issues—including crime, poverty, illegal immigration, health care, and environmental decline—are testing the nation's leaders. In the years ahead, politicians and citizens will face the challenges of maintaining prosperity in a global economy and in an increasingly volatile world.

The Statue of Liberty—known more formally as *Liberty Enlightening the World*—dominates the entrance to New York City's harbor. For immigrants who traveled to the United States by ship in the late 1800s and the 1900s, the huge copper sculpture was among their first glimpses of a new homeland.

A small lake sits amid the forests and steep mountains of Denali (formerly Mount McKinley) National Park in south central Alaska. Besides the gorgeous scenery, visitors come to see Denali—at 20,320 feet, the highest peak on the North American continent.

1) The Land

The United States, bordered in the east by the Atlantic Ocean and in the west by the Pacific Ocean, is the fourth largest country in the world. Only Russia, Canada, and China are larger in area. The mainland United States—which holds 48 of the nation's 50 states—spans the deserts, plains, and mountains of North America from east to west. To the north is Canada. Mexico and the Gulf of Mexico lie to the south. The states of Alaska and Hawaii lie at the northwestern edge of the continent and in the mid-Pacific Ocean, respectively.

The total area of the 50 states is nearly 3.8 million square miles, including coastal waters. Territories and possessions—such as Guam and American Samoa, in the Pacific Ocean, and Puerto Rico and the U.S. Virgin Islands in the Caribbean Sea—add about 12,000 square miles.

Topography

The United States has an extremely varied landscape, ranging from glaciers (slow-moving ice masses) to deserts. The mainland can be divided roughly into six geographical regions—the Atlantic Coastal Plain, the Appalachian Mountains, the Central Lowlands, the Great Plains, the

Intermountain Region, and the Cordillera, which includes Alaska. The state of Hawaii consists of both volcanic and coral islands.

ATLANTIC COASTAL PLAIN

The narrow Atlantic Coastal Plain curves along the shores of the Atlantic Ocean from the state of Massachusetts southward to the Gulf of Mexico. The oceanfront is made up mostly of wetlands (low, wet areas) and small islands. These barriers help to protect the coast from flooding during storms that blow in from the Atlantic Ocean. Estuaries (the mouths of rivers where freshwater and seawater mix) also line the coast and at certain points form natural ports such as New York, Boston, and Baltimore.

The Okefenokee Swamp (above), part of the narrow Atlantic Coastal Plain, straddles the border between Georgia and Florida. Farther north along the eastern seaboard is Martha's Vineyard (left), a resort island off the coast of Massachusetts.

Portions of the Atlantic Coastal Plain boast fertile and productive soils in which several of the nation's major crops are raised. For example, farmers grow much of the nation's citrus fruits in central Florida. In other sections of the Coastal Plain, however, the soil is naturally poor or nearly sterile from years of intensive farming.

APPALACHIAN MOUNTAINS

The Appalachians rise west of the Atlantic Coastal Plain. The continent's second longest mountain system, the low, rounded Appalachians extend from eastern Canada to Alabama. The Green and Catskill mountains belong to the northern Appalachians. Included among the central and southern ranges are the Blue Ridge and the Great Smoky mountains.

Appalachian farmers raise poultry, corn, tobacco, potatoes, and wheat in the valleys that lie between the ranges. Miners extract much of the nation's coal from the region's underground deposits.

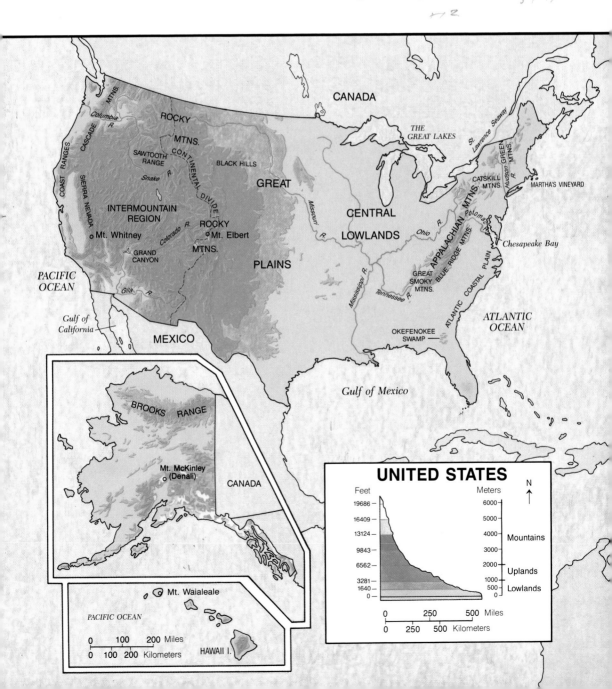

CENTRAL LOWLANDS

Often called the heartland of the United States, the Central Lowlands are located just west of the Appalachians and north of the southern section of the Atlantic Coastal Plain. Thousands of years ago, glaciers inched across the northern half of the Central Lowlands, sculpting the terrain and moving rocks and other debris. Most of the lowlands are flat, rarely rising more than 2,000 feet above sea level.

The glaciers also helped to create thousands of bodies of water, including the Great Lakes—Ontario, Huron, Erie, Michigan, and Superior—which make up the largest group of freshwater lakes in the world. Farther south, across the states of Iowa, Illinois, Indiana, and Ohio, the soils that developed on young glacial deposits proved very fertile. As a result, productive cropland now covers most of these states.

GREAT PLAINS

The Great Plains, a largely treeless region west of the Central Lowlands, reaches 4,000 feet above sea level. But the elevation only gradually increases, with large tracts of land appearing to be flat. About 500 miles wide, the Great Plains extend from Texas northward into Canada.

Photo by John R. Patton

Layers of fog shroud the peaks of the Great Smoky Mountains, a range in North Carolina that belongs to the Appalachians. This sprawling mountain system extends from eastern Canada southward through New England all the way to Alabama.

Included in the Central Lowlands is Lake Superior, the largest area of freshwater in the world. The lake, which measures 31,800 square miles, borders the U.S. states of Michigan, Minnesota, and Wisconsin and the Canadian province of Ontario.

Photo by Kay Shaw

Vast herds of American bison (buffalo) fed on the native grasses of the plains until the late 1800s, when settlers plowed the soil to plant wheat. This crop, along with the meat provided by millions of cattle and sheep, have helped to make the United States the world's leading agricultural nation. But drought and soil erosion in the plains have led to poor harvests or crop failures from time to time.

Courtesy of © Rick Jackson/Travel Montana

These lush wheat fields in central Montana grow at the northwestern edge of the Great Plains.

Sunshine dapples multicolored rock formations in Bryce Canyon National Park, a part of the Intermountain Region. Located in southern Utah, the park lies in an area of rugged uplands and steep canyons.

INTERMOUNTAIN REGION

The wide Intermountain Region consists mainly of rocky plateaus and bowl-shaped basins. These landforms dominate most of the states of Arizona, Nevada, and Utah and characterize eastern Oregon, western Wyoming, southern California, and southern Idaho, too.

In some places, the courses of rivers have eroded the plateaus to form buttes (isolated, flat-topped hills) and dramatically steep canyons. Long, low mountain ranges rise from the desert basins, which are the driest and hottest areas of the United States.

CORDILLERA

The Cordillera, a mountain system that borders the Great Plains in the east and the Pacific coast in the west, wraps around the Intermountain Region. The Rocky Mountains, part of the eastern Cordillera, run mostly north to south from Alaska and Canada to Mexico. This range boasts some of the tallest peaks in North America, including Mount Elbert (14,433 feet) in Colorado. The Continental Divide runs along the crest of the Rockies. The divide separates rivers that flow westward into the Pacific Ocean from those heading eastward into the Gulf of Mexico or the Atlantic Ocean.

The western Cordillera includes the Coast Ranges, the Sierra Nevada, and the Cascades. Several cities on the Pacific coast—including Portland, Oregon, and Sacramento, California—are situated in the valleys between these mountains.

Eastern sections of the Cordillera include many subranges of the Rocky Mountain system. These peaks in Idaho are part of the Sawtooth Range.

The Coast Ranges hug the nation's western shoreline, where huge underground plates overlap. Movement of the plates along fault lines jar these mountains and cause damaging earthquakes. The Sierra Nevada features Mount Whitney (14,494 feet), the highest peak of the mainland United States. North of the Sierra Nevada, the Cascades vary in elevation and include a number of active volcanoes.

ALASKA AND HAWAII

Separated from the mainland United States by Canada, Alaska—the nation's largest state—lies 500 miles northwest of Washington State. The Brooks Range, the northernmost section of the Rocky Mountains, runs through permanently frozen ground where no trees grow. The Coast Ranges of the Cordillera reach into southern Alaska, where Mount McKinley (Denali), the highest peak in North America, rises to an elevation of 20,320 feet.

Lying about 2,400 miles southwest of the mainland, the state of Hawaii is made up of eight major volcanic islands and more than 100 islets in the central Pacific Ocean. Some of these lush, tropical islands are actually large coral deposits. Other landmasses are the exposed tops of undersea volcanoes. The United States maintains several military bases on the islands, which also serve as ports for oceangoing vessels.

Photo by Buddy Mays/Travel Stock

Rivers

Waterways are vital to U.S. transportation, hydropower, irrigation, and daily water needs. The nation's major river systems are the Mississippi River—including its major connections to the Great Lakes-St. Lawrence Seaway—the Colorado River, and the Columbia River.

Courtesy of Dan Lerner

The sandy beaches and tropical climate of Hawaii attract visitors to this Pacific island state year-round.

13

From its source in northern Minnesota, the Mississippi River runs 2,348 miles southward through the central United States to New Orleans, Louisiana, on the Gulf of Mexico. Many of the waterways that lie east of the Continental Divide empty into the Mississippi or into one of its tributaries, which include the Ohio (and its feeder river, the Tennessee) and the Missouri. The entire system forms a key transportation network for U.S. goods.

The western United States has few navigable rivers. Dams on the largest waterways—including the Colorado and the Columbia—provide hydropower, irrigation, and flood control to the western part of the country.

Rising in the Rocky Mountains, the Colorado River meets the Gila River in Arizona before winding toward the Gulf of California, an arm of the Pacific Ocean. Along its long course, the Colorado passes through the Grand Canyon, a huge, steep-walled gorge.

The Columbia River flows for 1,214 miles from western Canada through the northwestern United States. In Idaho the waterway merges with its largest tributary, the Snake River, before emptying into the Pacific Ocean near Portland.

Climate

The climate in the United States varies greatly by region, elevation, and season. Most of the country, however, lies in the temperate zone of the Northern Hemisphere. Although moderate temperatures and precipitation are typical of the temperate zone, weather conditions can become extreme.

THE EASTERN MAINLAND

In the northeastern United States, summers are generally warm, and winters are cold. Average temperatures hover around 75° F throughout the summer months. During the winter, the northern states

Courtesy of Missouri Division of Tourism

Barges move huge amounts of cargo along the Mississippi River, which flows north to south in the central United States.

experience low temperatures. Madison, Wisconsin, for example, averages 14° F in January, the coldest month, while farther south in St. Louis, Missouri, winter temperatures reach an average of 40° F.

Warm air from the Gulf of Mexico keeps the weather mild in the southeastern mainland. Average winter readings vary from 45° F in Atlanta, Georgia, to 75° F in Key West, Florida, where the climate is tropical. Summers throughout the southeastern states are generally hot and muggy, with temperatures ranging anywhere from 75° F to 90° F.

Precipitation in the eastern half of the United States is highest along the Atlantic and Gulf coasts and also in the southern two-thirds of the interior. These areas usually receive about 70 inches of yearly precipitation. Moist air from the Gulf brings rain to the southern states in the winter. Every summer and fall, fierce hurricanes threaten the Gulf and Atlantic coasts. During the winter, cold air masses from Canada carry snow to the northern states. Here, the average annual precipitation is around 30 inches, but heavy snowfalls can deposit 12 or more inches at a time.

THE WESTERN MAINLAND

The Pacific Ocean, the Sierra Nevada, and the Cascades influence temperatures and precipitation in the western United States. The mountains trap the warm, moist air over the northwestern United States, where the blustering storms of the Pacific drop more than 80 inches of precipitation every year. In contrast, the mountains keep rainfall from reaching the deserts of the Intermountain Region, which gets less than 10 inches annually.

Winters on the western coast and in the southwest are generally mild. Average January temperatures range from 40° F in Seattle, Washington, to more than 60° F in Los Angeles, California. Farther inland, near Reno, Nevada, the temperature cools to below freezing.

East of the Rockies, warm air from the Gulf of Mexico and cold air from Canada sometimes clash, causing severe weather over the Great Plains. Blizzards, thunderstorms, and tornadoes often form suddenly in this region. In general the western Great Plains region is dry, averaging about 15 inches of precipitation a year. The eastern plains, however, experience humid conditions.

ALASKA AND HAWAII

Ocean currents and winds bring relatively mild weather to southern Alaska, where temperatures range from 20° F to 40° F in the winter and from 40° F to 60° F in the summer. But farther inland, average winter readings drop to 5° F. Typical summer temperatures are more agreeable, falling between 45° F and 75° F. At Point Barrow—Alaska's northernmost spot— temperatures are cool year-round. Summers average 45° F, and the long, cold winters experience chilly readings that dip to average lows of –12° F.

Precipitation, usually falling in the form of snow, is generally high along Alaska's southern coast. Average yearly precipitation exceeds 64 inches and has reached 220 inches in some spots. Levels drop sharply to 13 inches annually in the interior and to less than 8 inches in the far north.

In stark contrast to Alaska is the tropical state of Hawaii. Normal winter and summer temperatures differ by only a few degrees, from 72° F to 78° F. Mountainous areas of the islands are much cooler during the winter.

Precipitation throughout Hawaii varies considerably, partly because the state's mountains prevent rain clouds from reaching the lowlands. Mount Waialeale, one of the wettest places on earth, receives an average of 444 inches of rainfall a year. Honolulu, the state capital, gets 23 inches of rain annually, while Kawaihae, on the island of Hawaii, is dry, with less than 10 inches a year.

Sledding *(left)* is a favorite winter activity for people in northern states. In the summertime in southern California *(below),* families can view large-scale sandcastles sculpted by amateur artists.

Flora and Fauna

Forests of evergreens and stands of hardwood trees—such as oak, hickory, and walnut—dominate the eastern and north central sections of the United States. Bald cypress, tupelo, and white cedar trees grow in the swamps of the southeast. Fir trees, as well as redwoods and bristlecone pines, thrive in the west.

Before widespread settlement and plowing in the 1800s, tall prairie grasses and short steppe grasses covered most of the Great Plains. Native bluestem, grama, bunch, and buffalo grasses still remain but are limited in range. Tough desert plants of the Intermountain Region include cacti, yuccas, sagebrush, and mesquite. In contrast, the tropical zones of Hawaii and southern Florida sustain royal and thatch palms, which typically grow in warm, wet climates.

Animal species found throughout the nation include white-tailed deer, black bears, bobcats, beavers, coyotes, and snapping turtles. American bison, once nearly extinct, now roam wildlife preserves on the Great Plains. The Intermountain Region hosts thousands of reptiles, including the Gila monster, a poisonous lizard. The waters off the Pacific coast are home to sea lions, while manatees (sea cows) swim off the coast of Florida. The bald eagle, which was removed from the endangered species list in 1994, again flies throughout the United States, with the largest numbers in Alaska.

In the dry regions of the southwestern United States, saguaro cacti are majestic sights. The tallest cactus in the country, the saguaro can reach a height of 60 feet, and its blossom is the state flower of Arizona.

Independent Picture Service

Photo by Jerry Hennen

A bear cub clings to a tree in Vermont. Because of efforts to protect these animals, the number of bears in the United States has increased.

Natural Resources

The United States has a wide variety of natural resources, including minerals, trees, water, and soil. The country's most important resources are oil, natural gas, coal, and iron ore. Alaska, California, Texas, Louisiana, Oklahoma, and the Gulf of Mexico have productive oil fields, while coal is abundant in the Appalachian Mountains and in Wyoming.

Forests, which cover about one-third of the United States, supply the timber needed for newsprint, building materials, turpentine, and other wood products. Hardwood trees (primarily oak) of the Appalachians provide wood for the furniture industry. Softwoods, such as Douglas fir, are used mainly as lumber and make up 80 percent of the trees felled in the United States.

Photo by Erwin C. "Bud" Nielsen/Tucson, AZ

Autumn leaves color the forests of the Green Mountains, an Appalachian range that runs from Canada to Connecticut. Some of the trees supply wood to furniture makers in the region.

Blooming tulips brighten the cityscape of Washington, D.C., the nation's capital. Among the city's well-known landmarks are the Washington Monument *(pointed tower, center)*, the Lincoln Memorial *(left of tower)*, and the U.S. Capitol *(right of tower)*. These buildings lie in a line that follows the National Mall, a long, parklike area that gives residents open space amid the clusters of offices and historic structures.

Major Cities

The United States is highly urbanized, with 75 percent of the population living in cities and large towns. Eight U.S. cities have populations of more than one million, just within the city limits. The largest of these cities are New York, Los Angeles, Chicago, and Houston. The U.S. capital, Washington, D.C., has a smaller city population, but its crowded metropolitan area extends into Virginia and Maryland.

WASHINGTON, D.C.

The nation's capital since 1800, Washington, District of Columbia (metropolitan population 3.9 million), is named after President George Washington. Lying along the Potomac River between Virginia and Maryland, the capital is one of the few cities in the world that was planned before it was built. A French architect, Pierre Charles L'Enfant, laid out the city's streets, parks, and traffic circles.

As the headquarters of the national government, "the District" exists independently of any state. The city's buildings and memorials—including The White House, the U.S. Capitol, the Washington Monument, and the Lincoln Memorial— make Washington, D.C., a major tourist attraction. The federal government employs most of the area's workforce in service and administrative jobs.

NEW YORK CITY

New York (city population 7.3 million), one of the world's most important centers of business and culture, lies at the southeastern tip of New York State along the Hudson River. The city's beginnings date to 1624, when the Dutch established a settlement on what is now Manhattan Island.

In 1825 the opening of the Erie Canal in upstate New York provided the city with direct water access to states in the Great Lakes area. This new market for New York

The tall, matching towers of the World Trade Center in New York City dominate the urban skyline.

City's industrial goods helped its manufacturing sector to expand. As a result, the city's population grew rapidly throughout the 1800s, as immigrant jobseekers sailed from Europe across the Atlantic Ocean into New York's natural harbor.

Modern residents and visitors are attracted to New York for its world-famous theaters, museums, and monuments. Decisions made in the banks and stock exchanges that line Wall Street greatly impact the world's economy. At the United Nations headquarters building, diplomats from around the world try to resolve international conflicts.

LOS ANGELES

Sprawling across a desert basin in southern California, Los Angeles (city population 3.5 million) has grown rapidly since becoming a U.S. city in 1850. The first known settlement on the site was a Shoshone Indian village. By the late 1700s, Spaniards had begun to settle in the area, and in 1781 they founded the pueblo (town) of Los Angeles.

The city's population soared in the late 1800s, when low train fares brought thousands of settlers from the eastern United States. The basin's warm and dry climate also drew filmmakers in the early 1900s, and Los Angeles has since developed into a world-renowned movie capital.

Los Angeles has become the industrial, financial, and trading hub of the western United States. The manufacturing of aircraft and aerospace equipment, banking, the film industry, and tourism generate many of the city's jobs. The Port of Los Angeles, connected to the rest of the city by a narrow strip of land, is one of the world's finest artificial harbors and has docks for fishing boats, freighters, passenger liners, and small pleasure craft.

CHICAGO

Situated in northeastern Illinois on the southern shore of Lake Michigan, Chicago (city population 2.8 million) is the third largest city in the United States and the nation's leading overland transportation hub. In 1959, when the St. Lawrence Seaway opened up an all-water route from the Great Lakes to the Atlantic Ocean, Chicago also became a major seaport. Between its port, railroads, and trucking firms, Chicago now handles more freight than any other U.S. city. Chicago is also among the world's top industrial centers, manufacturing fabricated metals, foodstuffs, and many other products.

On the cultural side, Chicago is well known for its symphony orchestra as well as for its rhythm-and-blues bands. Architects and engineers study the city's buildings, many of which are examples of the Chicago School, a world-famous style of architecture that developed in the late 1800s.

HOUSTON

A leading shipping and oil-refining center, Houston (city population 1.6 million) lies about 50 miles inland from the Gulf of Mexico in southeastern Texas. The city is also home to the Lyndon B. Johnson Space Center, from which the National Aeronautics and Space Administration directs some of its space flights.

Founded in 1836, Houston is named after Sam Houston, who helped win Texas's independence from Mexico. The city's growth has stemmed from its location near the Gulf, as well as from the railroad tracks that connect Houston to other parts of Texas. Trains carry Texas farm products, such as cotton, to the Port of Houston to be shipped to other states. The discovery of oil in the Houston area has led major oil companies to establish refineries in the port city.

Courtesy of University of Houston

Downtown Houston is visible from the campus of the University of Houston.

Chaco Culture National Historical Park in New Mexico holds the remains of Pueblo Bonito, a large Anasazi Indian settlement that flourished from the tenth to about the twelfth century A.D. The village included a five-storied building that contained more than 1,000 rooms.

2) History and Government

About 20,000 years ago, nomadic hunters known as Paleo-Indians followed their prey across a land bridge that connected northern Asia with Alaska. These groups—ancestors of modern Native Americans—migrated far to the south and east, where they hunted mammoths, sloths, and bison across much of North America.

By 300 B.C., Indians who had gone as far south as Mexico had spread their farming skills to the nomadic peoples of the southern Intermountain Region. As they turned to crops for food, the Indians settled in permanent villages, some of which grew quite large. The Anasazi, for example, established Pueblo Bonito, one of the biggest such villages, in modern New Mexico in about the tenth century A.D.

At roughly the same time, in the Mississippi River valley and eastward, members of the Hopewell and the Mississippian cultures developed structured societies. They constructed huge earthen mounds in which to bury their dead and for this reason are also known as mound builders. These cultures eventually disappeared, but by the 1400s about 1.5 million Native Americans were living across the mid-continent. Their lifestyles and languages varied. Depending partly on what their environment offered, they farmed, hunted, fished, or gathered food.

Early European Explorations

In 1492, when the Italian explorer Christopher Columbus landed on the Bahamas (an island group east of Florida), he opened up a "New World" for Europe. Seafarers from Spain, France, and England soon followed Columbus to North America in search of gold and other valuables. The Europeans also wanted to find a quick and easy water route to Asia. But their explorations revealed that this so-called New World was bigger than they had ever imagined.

John Cabot, an Italian employed by England, sailed along the Atlantic coast as early as 1497. Although Cabot claimed the shores for England, the English monarchs waited a century before establishing settlements in North America.

The Spaniards were the first Europeans to explore the seemingly limitless landmass that lay beyond the eastern coastline. Juan Ponce de León landed in what is now Florida in 1513, and in 1539 Hernando de Soto searched for gold from Florida to the Mississippi River. Francisco Coronado ventured from Mexico as far north as present-day Kansas and Colorado. Their travels allowed Spain to claim huge sections of North America.

Meanwhile, the French sent Giovanni da Verrazano to the Atlantic coast. Later French explorers pushed westward through the Great Lakes and toward the Mississippi River. René-Robert Cavalier de La Salle followed the river southward to its mouth at the Gulf of Mexico. In 1682 he claimed the entire Mississippi River region—which he named the Louisiana Territory—for France. The new French domain stretched westward from the Mississippi River to the Rocky Mountains.

Colonization

To strengthen their land claims, the English and the Spanish tried to set up settlements. In 1565 Pedro Menéndez de Avilés established the first permanent European town in what is now the United States at St. Augustine, Florida. In 1607 the English founded Jamestown, Virginia, where the inhabitants barely survived disease, famine, and attacks by local

Courtesy of Historical Pictures relating to the Louisiana Purchase issued by the *St. Louis Globe-Democrat*, 1902

In a historical painting, a captured Indian guide (near horse's head) **shows the Spanish explorer Hernando de Soto** (on horseback) **where he and his men can cross the Mississippi River. De Soto landed in what became the United States in 1539, searching for gold and claiming territories for Spain.**

Indians. The Dutch gained their foothold in the early 1600s, when they hired the Englishman Henry Hudson to explore what is now New York State. His findings led the Dutch to organize trading settlements in New Netherland (modern New York City). The colony, funded by the Dutch West India Company, prospered by selling beaver pelts to the European market.

At the same time, religious sects seeking freedom of worship began to arrive from Europe. In 1620 Pilgrims from England established Plymouth (now in Massachusetts), the first colony in what came to be called New England. Shortly afterward, Puritans founded the colonies of Rhode Island, Connecticut, and Massachusetts Bay (which later merged with Plymouth).

By the early 1700s, England had become part of the United Kingdom of Great Britain. The expanded realm included 13 colonies along the Atlantic coast. Protected by the British navy and supplied by British merchant ships, these colonies attracted settlers from Britain, Ireland, the Netherlands, Germany, France, and Sweden. The newcomers held fast to their various languages, religions, and cultures.

Along with European settlement came European diseases that devastated the Native Americans of the eastern coast. Many of these and other Indian groups were pushed westward as the number of colonists grew steadily. By the mid-1700s, the white population of British America had reached nearly two million. The importation of black slaves from Africa added

A group of Pilgrims (members of a religious sect that set up a colony in Massachusetts) make their way to services in the early 1600s. Venturing from Britain, the Pilgrims sought a place where they would be free to practice their own form of the Christian faith.

Some Indians fought alongside the French against Britain in the French and Indian War (1755–1763). British commanders were not familiar with the local methods of warfare, such as the ambush (surprise raid), and lost key battles as a result. In the end, however, the British defeated the French and gained French colonial territories as part of the postwar peace settlement.

Courtesy of Library of Congress

about 500,000 inhabitants. In some colonies, the slaves outnumbered their owners, who used the slaves to work large plantations.

Unlike the British, the French had always been more interested in trading than in establishing colonies. French traders maintained peaceful relations with many of the Indians in North America, exchanging goods for valuable beaver pelts.

But in the 1700s, British colonists began to venture into French commercial areas, and clashes erupted. The last of these conflicts triggered the decisive French and Indian War (1754–1763), in which the French and the British fought over land claims in North America. To limit Britain's power, Spain and many Indian nations allied with the French. But France lost the war and nearly all of its land in North America. Most French colonial territory went to Britain. France ceded (gave up) the Louisiana Territory to Spain.

Achieving Independence

The end of the French and Indian War did not bring peace to North America. To protect the fur trade and to defend colonists against possible Indian attacks, Britain's king sent 10,000 troops to the 13 colonies. To pay for the soldiers' food, clothing, and salaries, the king heavily taxed the colonies. The taxes met fierce resistance from colonists, who protested that only their own elected assemblies could enact such measures.

Armed encounters between colonists and the British navy eventually convinced the king to repeal most of the taxes. But many of the colonists in Massachusetts and elsewhere had already come to favor full independence. This trend encouraged the British to blockade Boston's harbor in 1774 to prevent colonial merchants from exporting goods.

In response, leaders from throughout the colonies gathered at the first Continental

To help Britain pay for waging the French and Indian War, the British government taxed its 13 North American colonies. Thomas Jefferson (left), a farmer and landowner in the colony of Virginia, strongly opposed the taxes and shared his views with leaders in other colonies. By 1775 many colonists were fed up with British rule, and in the next year Jefferson wrote the Declaration of Independence to announce the colonies' break with Britain. Colonial troops (below) marched from Dover, Delaware, to fight Britain's forces in the American War of Independence (1775–1783).

Congress in Philadelphia, Pennsylvania. The king ignored the congress's plea to change commercial and taxation policies, and so the colonies refused to buy their goods from Britain. After unsuccessfully urging Britain to withdraw its troops, the congress advised the people of Massachusetts to prepare for war.

The first clash of the American War of Independence (1775–1783) took place in Massachusetts, where colonial and British soldiers met in short skirmishes. Many colonists felt that the colonies could not defeat the British, who maintained one of the world's strongest armies as well as a powerful navy. Other colonists—including John Adams, George Washington, and Thomas Paine—supported rebellion. In 1776 Paine published Common Sense, a pamphlet that inspired thousands to reject British rule and to choose independence.

As public support for the rebellion increased, the Continental Congress raised a Continental army and asked George Washington to lead it. On July 4, 1776, the congress passed the Declaration of Independence. This document justified the revolt on the grounds that the British had failed to protect the basic rights and freedoms of the colonists. The declaration marked the colonies' official break with British rule.

Washington's army suffered from a lack of supplies and training, and the British defeated the colonists in Boston, New York, and Philadelphia. But in 1777 a colonial victory at Saratoga, New York, convinced France to ally with the colonists against Britain—France's longtime enemy. This alliance changed the outcome of the war.

In 1781 a colonial militia forced the British to retreat to Yorktown, Virginia, to await more troops and supplies. But after the French navy turned back the British reinforcements, Washington stormed Yorktown and defeated its garrison. The loss convinced British leaders that their side could not win the war. In 1783 the British signed the Treaty of Paris, recognizing the former 13 colonies as the independent United States of America. The new nation took possession of all British territory from the Atlantic coast westward to the Mississippi River.

Conflict and Expansion

Before the war ended, the Continental Congress had drawn up the Articles of Confederation, which described the future government of the colonies. In 1787 leaders from the former colonies, now called states, met in Philadelphia to expand and improve the articles.

Under the new document, or Constitution, a president—not a hereditary monarch—would lead the nation. A legislature called a congress would make the nation's laws, which could be vetoed (rejected) by the president. Each former British colony had to ratify (approve) the Constitution to be admitted into the United States of America. In 1789 voters elected George Washington as the nation's first president.

In the early nineteenth century, the new country faced the problems of westward expansion and further conflict with Britain. In 1801, during the Napoleonic Wars in Europe, France regained control of the Louisiana Territory. The French leader Napoleon Bonaparte sold it to the United

Courtesy of Picture Division, Public Archives of Canada, Ottawa

After the war ended in 1783, citizens of the new United States of America turned to commerce. Here, boatmen rest beside a river during a trip into Canada, where furs were the main item of trade.

States two years later. This transaction, called the Louisiana Purchase, doubled the size of the United States and extended its western boundary from the Mississippi River to the Rocky Mountains.

At the same time, the United States was expanding its commercial links to Europe. But overseas trade became a source of conflict between Britain and the United States during the early 1800s. The Napoleonic Wars between Britain and France hurt overseas trade, which was crucial to the U.S. economy. To stop U.S. supplies from reaching France, the British seized U.S. merchant ships in European waters. In addition, the British kidnapped U.S. sailors and forced them to serve in the British navy.

Congress called for the United States to go to war against Britain. Members were angry about the seizure of U.S. ships and sailors, actions that also fostered anti-British public opinion. One of the strongest motives for the war, however, was to stop Britain from supplying guns to the Indians. The British had been trying to prevent U.S. expansion by providing Native American groups in western lands with weapons to use against settlers.

The United States declared war on Britain in 1812. The two nations fought several battles in the Atlantic Ocean and in the Great Lakes area. The British even attacked Washington, D.C., the U.S. capital. In 1814 Britain signed a peace treaty with the United States. Neither country claimed victory nor admitted defeat.

Continental and Economic Growth

In the decades following the War of 1812, millions of traders, soldiers, and settlers moved west of the Appalachians in search of land and adventure. To encourage settlement, the U.S. government built forts that served as supply depots and as bases from which soldiers could attack Indians trying to prevent U.S. expansion. To pro-

In 1803 the United States bought the Louisiana Territory from France. President Thomas Jefferson sent a team *(right)* that included the explorers Meriwether Lewis and William Clark to chart the new territory, which stretched past the Rockies to the Pacific coast and doubled the size of the country. To aid them in finding their way over the enormous, unmapped area, the team had the help of Sacagawea *(center),* a young Shoshone Indian woman.

Courtesy of Woolaroc Museum, Bartlesville, Oklahoma

After the Lewis and Clark expedition, white settlers began to push westward. This movement brought the newcomers into conflict with Native Americans, who had long lived in lands throughout the United States. By the 1830s, the U.S. government was forcing Indian groups to travel from their traditional homes to Indian Territory (now in Oklahoma), which was part of the Louisiana Purchase.

mote more westward movement, the U.S. government divided its western landholdings into territories. When a territory's population reached 60,000, it could apply for statehood.

The growing demand for rich farmland prompted the U.S. government to buy or take land from Indians who lived in the territories. In the 1830s, the government forced the Creek, Chickasaw, Cherokee, Seminole, and Choctaw peoples to move hundreds of miles westward to a reservation called Indian Territory (now mostly in Oklahoma). Hundreds of Indians died along the route, which became known as the Trail of Tears.

Meanwhile, the industrial states of the northern United States (collectively called the North) saw rapid economic growth as new factories in the region produced goods for an expanding market. This Industrial Revolution greatly changed economic and social conditions. Instead of sewing clothing or making tools in the home, workers now labored in factories, where they used heavy machinery to produce large quantities of consumer goods. Many farmers soon left their fields for better-paying jobs in cities. Millions of jobless immigrants, mainly from Europe, also flocked to industrial centers, such as New York, Boston, and Philadelphia.

The invention of steamboats and railroads in the first half of the nineteenth century allowed goods to be transported from the northeast to expanding markets in the western territories and states. The Erie Canal linked the Atlantic states with the Great Lakes region, where rapidly increasing populations also needed goods.

Farther west, hundreds of U.S. citizens and immigrants were moving to territories claimed by Mexico. Some of these newcomers drew up their own laws in defiance of the Mexican government. These actions led to the Mexican War (1846–1848), which the United States won. The peace treaty that ended the conflict gave the United States the Mexican territories now called Texas, New Mexico, Colorado, Utah, and

Courtesy of Denver Public Library, Western History Department

The shallowness of the Snake River in Idaho allowed wagons and horses to cross safely in the 1840s, when immigrants and U.S. citizens made the long journey across the Rocky Mountains to the Pacific coast.

California. The United States spanned North America from the Atlantic to the Pacific.

In 1848, shortly after the Mexican War, miners found gold in California. The discovery drew thousands of people to the Pacific coast. By 1850 white settlers made up nearly 70 percent of California's population, greatly outnumbering the Mexicans and Indians, who had lived there before U.S. independence.

Civil War and Reconstruction

The economy of the industrial North was linked in many ways to the more agricultural economy of the southern states (collectively called the South). Northern cloth mills, for example, depended on the cotton grown on large southern plantations that used slave labor. Slavery, however, had been outlawed in the North.

Southern plantation owners reasoned that they could not produce cotton at a profit unless they had slave labor. Some northerners argued that slavery was cruel and immoral and should be abolished (made illegal) throughout the United States. This issue led to conflict between abolitionist states and slave-owning states.

When Abraham Lincoln, a northerner, was elected president in November 1860, the conflict over slavery worsened. Knowing that Lincoln wanted to prohibit slavery in new territories, the southern state of South Carolina seceded (left) the United States in December 1860. By 1861 a total of 11 southern states had seceded and had formed the Confederate States of America.

To keep the United States together, Lincoln sent 75,000 soldiers to the South. By the spring of 1861, the Civil War had broken out. Union soldiers from the North fought the Confederate forces of the South. The two huge armies clashed for four years in dozens of bloody battles, including Bull Run, Antietam, and Shiloh. The fighting killed and wounded hundreds of thousands of soldiers on both sides and destroyed cities, towns, and farms in the South.

To end the war, Lincoln threatened to use his executive authority to free the southern slaves unless the South surrendered. The South refused to give in. On January 1, 1863, Lincoln's Emancipation Proclamation liberated thousands of black men, women, and children. Many of the men joined the Union's forces.

Without slave labor to raise crops for export, the South slowly ran out of money and supplies. By 1864—after three years of stalemate—the North began to gain the upper hand. Eventually, most Confederate leaders became convinced that continuing the war would be futile. On April 9, 1865, Union general Ulysses S. Grant accepted the surrender of Confederate general Robert E. Lee.

30

Some U.S. states, mostly in the South, allowed farmers to own black slaves whose ancestors had been brought from Africa in the 1700s. Other states, mainly in the North, had outlawed slavery. By the 1860s, the North and the South were so opposed to one another's beliefs that Civil War had broken out. During the conflict, which lasted from 1861 to 1865, soldiers on both sides fought hand to hand in the Battle of Atlanta *(above)* in Georgia. In 1863 President Abraham Lincoln *(right)* used the power of his office to free the slaves in Confederate states in the hope of forcing them to surrender. His plan did not work at first, and the war dragged on, causing widespread destruction to the southern states.

31

From 1865 to 1877, a period known as Reconstruction, the U.S. government rebuilt the South. To be readmitted to the Union, each southern state that had seceded had to ratify the Fourteenth Amendment to the Constitution. The amendment (change) stated that all people born in the United States, including former slaves, were U.S. citizens.

The South's recovery proved difficult. The war had ravaged the region's farms, had blown up its railways, and had ruined its buildings and bridges. The national government rebuilt cities, relaid railroad tracks, repaired schools, and returned people to work. Federal troops patrolled the southern states to keep order.

But the local governments that came to power during Reconstruction were eventually controlled by a combination of northerners, southerners who had supported the Union, and former slaves. Most southerners did not fall into any of these categories and resented being represented by people who had once been considered the enemy.

As southern whites regained power, they directed their resentment at the region's black population. Local officials, for instance, enacted laws that made it difficult for black people to vote or to receive an education. Secret, radical groups, such as the Ku Klux Klan, terrorized blacks with beatings and hangings. These actions often had the support of Klan-controlled local governments.

The Western Frontier

During and after the Civil War, the U.S. government offered free land in the western territories to people who would settle there. This policy brought a rush of land-hungry settlers to the plains and mountains of the western United States. Some people even moved as far as Alaska, which the United States had purchased from Russia in 1867.

Courtesy of Library of Congress

The formation of the Ku Klux Klan, a secret society of white people, dates to the end of the Civil War. Defeated southern soldiers established the Klan and used violence to stop blacks and other minorities from exercising their civil rights. To hide their identities, Klan members often wore robes and pointed hoods.

32

In the late 1800s, passengers on the Union Pacific Railroad shot at herds of bison as the trains traveled through the Great Plains. In 1870 the number of these huge animals—the main food source for the Plains Indians—stood at roughly 7,000,000. About a decade later, lack of food and sport killing had reduced the number to around 200.

Members of the Cree and the Chippewa (or Ojibwa) tribes posed in 1896 in Montana, where the two groups shared land on an Indian reservation.

Nineteenth-century settlers in this Nebraska homestead lived in a dugout dwelling made of sod.

Throughout the western United States in the late 1800s, cowboys watched over vast herds of livestock. A cowboy usually did not own his horse, but rather rode one of several mounts that belonged to his boss—the rancher. The rope, or lariat, was a cowboy's most important tool, and he used it to catch a fleeing cow by tossing it over the animal's neck, horns, or legs.

Most people believed that Indians and U.S. citizens could not live peacefully side by side. To extend its control of the western frontier, the government pushed more and more Indians onto reservations. Farmers who came in their place plowed much of the Great Plains, substituting crops for the region's native grasses, which had once supported vast herds of bison. Sport hunters shot thousands of the big animals on which Indian nations had long depended. As bison dwindled, the Indians lost their main means of support and decreased in number from lack of food. By 1890 U.S. troops had moved or subdued most of the remaining Indians. These actions opened the western lands to unhindered settlement and development.

The expansion of the nation's railway system also reduced Indian use of traditional lands. As more settlers headed westward, small towns developed along wagon trails and railroad lines. The towns became commercial centers for crops, livestock, and other goods. Farmers, ranchers, and cowboys brought crops, cattle, and sheep to the towns to be shipped to eastern markets.

Industrialization

While the western settlement continued, a growing transportation system and the country's vast natural resources led to explosive economic growth. Eastern factories supplied iron and steel for the sprawling railway network, for machinery, and for the construction industry. Textile mills provided cloth for factories to sew into clothing. Lumber, coal, and petroleum businesses also benefited from the nation's industrialization.

The factories employed a large labor force, but often there were more jobs open than people to fill them. The availability of jobs resulted in a wave of immigrant workers. Between 1890 and 1914, about 16 million immigrants—mostly from Russia, Poland, Italy, and Greece—entered the United States looking for work and a better life.

Courtesy of North Carolina Division of Archives and History

At a textile mill in North Carolina, a floor manager shows a young girl how to monitor spools of thread. As the United States became more industrialized, the number of factories increased. In need of a larger workforce, many businesses used child labor.

Courtesy of Library of Congress

The opportunity to find a job brought many poor immigrants from Europe to the United States. A section of New York City became the home of thousands of newcomers from Italy, and the area was later dubbed "Little Italy."

In the factories, many adult and child laborers toiled for 10 or 12 hours a day for low wages. Entire families sometimes worked just to pay for food and clothing and to rent rooms in poorly maintained apartment buildings. As business owners grew increasingly wealthy, the gap between rich and poor widened, leading to civil and labor unrest.

By the end of the nineteenth century, U.S. business leaders had created several monopolies (industries that are completely dominated by single corporations). The largest monopolies centered around the railroad, steel, and petroleum industries. Because a monopoly had no competition, its owner could charge customers high prices for goods or services. To avoid regulation by the government, many monopolies bribed local, state, and national legislators.

From the late 1890s to the early 1900s, reformers set out to correct the various problems caused by rapid industrialization, population growth, and widespread corruption. These reformers initiated legislation to regulate monopolies and to enforce child labor laws.

Foreign Involvement

Throughout these decades of growth and change, the United States had largely stayed out of foreign affairs. Some U.S. citizens felt the country should use its power and wealth to acquire territories rich in natural resources. Many other people maintained that the nation should avoid foreign entanglements. Wars and negotiations in the late 1800s changed the U.S. policy of noninvolvement and brought several new lands into U.S. hands.

A historical drawing depicts an explosion ripping through the U.S.S. *Maine* in 1898 in Havana, Cuba. The sinking of the ship and the resulting loss of life brought the United States into conflict with Spain, which claimed Cuba as a colony. Although the Spanish-American War lasted only four months, the United States thereafter increasingly used its military and economic power on the world scene.

Black clouds of airborne soil pursue a car as it speeds through Nebraska during the 1930s. Strong winds and drought had loosened the region's topsoil, which often traveled thousands of miles from where it originated. As a result of the dust storms, many farms in the Great Plains could no longer grow crops and were abandoned.

After its 1898 victory in the Spanish-American War, the United States seized the former Spanish colonies of Cuba, Puerto Rico, Guam, and the Philippine Islands. In that same year, the United States also took over the Hawaiian Islands at the urging of U.S. businesspeople, who wanted U.S. leaders to set up favorable shipping laws in the Pacific region.

During World War I (1914–1918), the United States remained neutral until 1917, when German submarines attacked several U.S. merchant ships in the Atlantic Ocean. The United States entered the war on the side of France and Britain, sending two million troops and massive supplies of arms overseas to defeat Germany.

After the war, the United States enjoyed a decade of prosperity. Expanding U.S. industries produced cars, refrigerators, and washing machines. The economic boom ended in 1929, with the crash of the New York stock market—a worldwide economic investment center. Investors lost money, factories closed, and jobs disappeared.

The long downturn, known as the Great Depression, worsened in rural areas where droughts and strong winds killed crops and blew away fertile topsoil. Thousands of farmers on the Great Plains abandoned their land and moved from the region.

To combat the depression, U.S. president Franklin D. Roosevelt initiated the New Deal in the 1930s. This series of government-funded programs provided food, money, and jobs to millions of unemployed people. The New Deal helped for a while, and Roosevelt's widespread popularity allowed him to win election four times in a row.

In the late 1930s, war again threatened many parts of Europe. Factories in the United States reopened to make weapons and other heavy goods. The U.S. military added ships, tanks, and other equipment to its arsenal, a move that also helped manufacturing. The upturn in production ended the depression and prepared the nation for World War II (1939–1945).

On December 7, 1941, smoke and flames billowed from bomb-damaged planes. The bombs were part of the surprise Japanese attack on the port of Pearl Harbor in the Hawaiian Islands. Because of the raid, the United States joined Britain, France, and other countries in fighting against Japan and Germany in World War II (1939–1945).

Most people in the United States did not want to go to war again. The Allies (including Canada, Britain, France, China, and later the Soviet Union) were fighting the Axis powers of Germany, Italy, and Japan. On December 7, 1941, however, Japan bombed Pearl Harbor, a U.S. naval base in the Hawaiian Islands. The next day, the United States declared war on Japan, and Germany and Italy soon joined Japan's effort to defeat the United States.

Clashes in the Pacific and in Europe cost many U.S. lives, as U.S. soldiers, sailors, and marines took part in sea and land battles. Ships ferried a huge armada of U.S. supplies to faraway places in Asia, Africa, and Europe. Allied leaders planned a variety of strategies to defeat the Axis nations, including a massive invasion of German-occupied France in 1944. Italy soon withdrew from the war, and Germany gave up in May 1945. To force Japan's

surrender, the United States destroyed two Japanese cities with deadly atomic bombs in August 1945.

After the war ended, the United States and the Soviet Union emerged as the world's two superpowers. The Soviet Union had long been spreading its Communist political and economic system to other countries. (Under Communism, one group controls the economy, education, government, and the media.) The United States, which favored free markets and private ownership, established a policy to stop Communism from taking hold in other countries.

To strengthen its influence, the United States set up the North Atlantic Treaty Organization (NATO), a military alliance of mostly western European nations. In response, the Soviet Union and its allies in central and eastern Europe signed a similar treaty called the Warsaw Pact.

Years of Conflict

In the decades after World War II, the United States and the Soviet Union became rivals in a weapons race. Each side built up arsenals of nuclear arms and stationed forces in Europe. The United States also gave military support to countries trying to prevent a Communist regime from gaining power. This policy of intervention involved the United States in the Korean War (1950–1953) and the Vietnam War (1955–1975).

Meanwhile, people in the United States were fighting battles on the homefront. Led by activists such as Dr. Martin Luther King, Jr., African Americans protested racial segregation, which barred minority populations from equal opportunities in jobs, education, housing, and other areas.

Courtesy of National Archives

In 1963 Dr. Martin Luther King, Jr., an African American civil rights activist, addressed a crowd of more than 200,000 people in Washington, D.C. *(right)*. His stirring speech was a plea for racial equality for all the nation's people of color. U.S. troops *(below)* guarded African American students in Arkansas as they entered a school that had once barred them from attendance.

Courtesy of *Arkansas Democrat-Gazette*

39

The current version of the U.S. flag came into use in 1960, when the fiftieth star was added to signify the inclusion of Hawaii. The 13 stripes stand for the original states that formed the United States in the late 1700s.

Artwork by Laura Westlund

The protests, which sometimes became violent, eventually brought change. In 1954, for example, the U.S. Supreme Court ruled to desegregate public schools. In 1964 Congress passed the Civil Rights Act, making it illegal to discriminate against blacks and other minorities.

Another group—antiwar protesters—expressed their views in large student demonstrations, where they vocalized their opposition to U.S. involvement in Vietnam. In time the students were joined by people of all economic, ethnic, and social levels in demanding that the United States pull

In 1968 Chicago hosted the national convention of the Democratic party—one of the two main political groups in the United States. Among hotly debated topics both inside and outside the convention hall was U.S. involvement in the Vietnam War (1955–1975). Here, members of the Illinois National Guard face crowds of antiwar protesters.

Photo by United Press International

out of the conflict. By 1973 the government had withdrawn all U.S. troops from Vietnam.

Amid this turmoil arose a political scandal. President Richard M. Nixon was charged with misconduct during his bid for reelection. The scandal forced Nixon to resign in 1974—a decision no previous president had ever had to make.

The economy also became a major concern during the late 1970s, when high oil prices and rising inflation slowed growth and hampered investment. In 1981, to stimulate economic activity, Congress enacted the largest income-tax cut in U.S. history. Inflation dropped, but tax revenues declined. The government, which still needed money for the weapons race, began to spend more than it earned in taxes. This policy led to an unprecedented growth in the nation's budget deficit (shortfall in income) that continued into the 1990s.

Recent Events

The United States was not the only superpower with problems. In the early 1990s, Warsaw Pact governments faced successful revolts against their Communist systems. The rebellions contributed to the collapse of the Soviet Union. This ended the arms race and left the United States as the world's sole superpower—in both economic and military terms.

The shift also intensified the U.S. role in foreign affairs. In 1991, for example, the United States led an international coalition against Iraq after Iraq invaded Kuwait, an oil-rich U.S. ally. On the African continent, U.S. troops brought humanitarian relief to Somalia. In 1993 U.S. military planes dropped food and medical supplies to occupied cities in the European country of Bosnia-Herzegovina—a former Yugoslav republic torn by civil war. In 1994, U.S. troops helped exiled president Jean-Bertrand Aristide return to power in the Caribbean nation of Haiti.

In addition to flexing its military and political muscle, the United States is a major player in the global economy and strives to keep up in an increasingly competitive marketplace. In the early 1990s, U.S. leaders helped to lift trade barriers

Courtesy of United Nations High Commissioner for Refugees

In the early 1990s, U.S. troops supported the effort of the United Nations to protect Kurdish refugees in the Middle Eastern nation of Iraq. The Kurds, an ethnic minority living there, had fled northward during and after the Persian Gulf War between Iraq and the neighboring country of Kuwait.

between the United States, Canada, and Mexico by passing the North American Free Trade Agreement (NAFTA). The treaty ended the payment of tariffs (taxes) to member-nations on imports and exports. Another multinational treaty—the General Agreement on Tariffs and Trade—passed through Congress in 1994. The treaty lowers or removes taxes on thousands of products bought and sold worldwide.

Domestic issues—including violent crime, urban gangs, poverty, welfare, racial tension, homelessness, illegal immigration, and health-care reform—were major U.S. concerns in the mid-1990s. These issues most likely will occupy politicians and citizens for years to come. The United States remains an economic and military superpower, but its people and its leaders are divided over the best way to improve conditions both at home and abroad.

Government

The government of the United States was the first to be based on a written constitution, which sets forth the powers of the national and state governments. Under

Beginning in the 1970s, groups pushed the U.S. government to pay more attention to environmental problems. Most administrations were slow to act. In 1992, however, President Bill Clinton made the environment a bigger priority. Here, with his vice president Al Gore looking on, he explains a new initiative on global climate change.

President George Washington laid the cornerstone for the U.S. Capitol in 1793, and Congress first met in the domed building in 1800. The wing for the House of Representatives extends to the south of the domed section, and the Senate wing stretches to the north. Renovations have not changed the basic design, which was the work of an amateur architect named William Thornton.

this system, the national (federal) government can only exercise powers outlined or implied in the U.S. Constitution. All 50 states can use the powers given to them in the Constitution and can assume powers that do not conflict with the Constitution.

The Constitution provides for three federal branches of government—executive, legislative, and judicial—that are designed to work together to run the country. This separation of powers gives each branch some independence and balances the federal government.

The executive branch includes the president, the vice president, and the heads of executive offices such as the Department of State and the Office of Management and Budget. The president is the chief executive officer and chief of state, whose main responsibilities include enforcing federal laws, appointing federal officials, commanding the armed forces, and conducting foreign affairs. The vice president replaces the president if the president dies, resigns, or is removed from office. Both leaders are elected jointly for a four-year term and cannot be reelected more than once.

The legislative branch of government is represented by Congress, which is divided into the Senate and the House of Representatives. Congress is responsible for making, repealing, and amending federal laws. The Senate, which approves federal appointments and international treaties, has 100 members—2 from each state—who serve six-year terms. The number of representatives a state sends to the House is determined by the state's population. As a result, the number of congresspeople fluctuates according to changes in population and in population distribution.

The judicial branch is made up of the U.S. Supreme Court, 95 federal district courts, and 12 federal courts of appeal. With Senate approval, the president appoints the nine judges of the Supreme Court, who serve for life. The Supreme Court, the highest court in the nation, hears cases that involve foreign countries or more than one state. Cases heard on a lower level may be appealed to the Supreme Court, which can decline to accept them. The Supreme Court also handles cases that ensure state and federal governments stay within the boundaries of the Constitution.

Each state government is also divided into executive, legislative, and judicial branches. The elected state governor executes state laws, appoints state officials, commands the state militia, and oversees preparation of the state budget. Most states have a bicameral (two-house) legislature. States have courts with limited jurisdiction, and most have state supreme courts.

On a warm day, the beach at Coney Island, a section of New York City, is a sea of umbrellas and sunbathers.

3) The People

By the mid-1990s, the population of the United States had reached nearly 261 million. The nation's average population density—71 persons per square mile—does not reflect the actual distribution of people. Sections of the northeast and the Pacific coast are heavily populated. The central United States, the mountainous regions, Alaska, and Hawaii hold fewer people.

Ethnic and Religious Mixture

Most newcomers to what became the United States were from Spain and Britain.

By the 1800s, French, German, and Scandinavian peoples were crossing the Atlantic Ocean in search of political freedom and economic opportunity. Immigrants from nations in eastern Europe and southern Europe made up a growing percentage of urban populations in the late 1800s and early 1900s. As a result of these trends, about three-fourths of the U.S. population is now white with European ancestry.

Descendants of Africans who had been brought to the United States as slaves before the Civil War now account for 12 percent of the population. Some black

Native Americans make up a small part of the total U.S. population. Many Indians hold fast to their ancient traditions through language, music, and religious practices.

immigrants have arrived more recently from Africa and Latin America.

Latinos—people who came from or who are descendants of immigrants from Latin America—make up 9 percent of the overall U.S. population. Most Latinos in the United States arrived from Mexico, Cuba, and Central America.

About 3 percent of the U.S. population claims ancestry from China, India, Vietnam, Laos, Cambodia, Japan, Korea, or the

Young girls participate in Afram, an African American festival celebrated in Maryland. Many of the participants dress in African-style clothing and learn about everyday traditions of Africa's many ethnic groups. Throughout the continent, for example, girls and women carry baskets by balancing them on their heads.

45

Some religious faiths that people practice in the United States developed within the country. Brigham Young *(left)*, for example, helped to found the Church of Jesus Christ of Latter-day Saints (the Mormon Church) in the 1800s. Newcomers to the United States, on the other hand, have brought their age-old religions with them. These Middle Eastern immigrants *(right)* are praying together at a mosque (Islamic house of prayer) in Michigan. Islam originated on the Arabian Peninsula in the seventh century A.D.

Philippines. The ancestry of many Asian American families dates to the mid-1800s, when people from eastern Asia came to work on the U.S. railway system. Recently, hundreds of thousands of Asians have emigrated to the United States, making Asia one of the largest sources of immigrants in the 1990s.

Only 1 percent of the population is Native American. Many Native Americans live on reservations, most of which are located in the western half of the country.

Because the United States consists of one of the world's most diverse populations, the nation has been referred to as a melting pot—a place where different ethnic groups have adopted a common culture. Most people speak English, wear similar fashions, and enjoy the same types of recreation. On the other hand, many groups strive to maintain their cultural identities, speaking their own languages, organizing traditional festivals, and attending their own religious services.

More than 1,000 different religious groups exist in the United States. Some sects—including Seventh-day Adventists, Church of Jesus Christ of Latter-day Saints (Mormons), Jehovah's Witnesses, and Christian Scientists—were founded in the United States. Other religions were brought by immigrants from Europe, Asia, and the Middle East.

Nearly 60 percent of the nation's citizens are members of an organized religion, and most of these believers are Christians.

About 38 percent of the population who claim a religious tie belong to the Roman Catholic Church—the largest single denomination in the United States.

Protestants, whose sects originated in sixteenth-century Europe, make up another 52 percent. The largest Protestant sects are Baptist, Methodist, and Lutheran. Jews, Mormons, Muslims (followers of the Islamic faith), and members of various Eastern Orthodox churches sustain smaller but substantial religious communities. Although the U.S. government does not support any church, the predominantly Christian population has influenced government actions, including the selection of some national holidays.

Health and Education

The United States maintains an extensive network of public and private hospitals and health clinics. Private companies as well as employees provide health insurance. Insurance for the elderly and the unemployed is available through government programs. In addition, many public health departments offer immunizations, laboratory tests, and other services to help prevent the spread of diseases such as tuberculosis.

Cancer and heart disease are among the most common and deadly diseases afflicting people in the United States. The country is also struggling to combat acquired immune deficiency syndrome (AIDS). To

A nurse tends to the needs of a young patient in an emergency room. The United States offers a wide variety of services in its health-care system. Government-run programs provide some services, while others are covered by private insurance.

Photo by Bob and Diane Wolfe

prevent the spread of the illness, federal and state governments have launched campaigns to educate the public about AIDS prevention and testing.

The average life expectancy of people born in the United States is 76 years, which is equal to or slightly lower than the figures for other developed countries. The nation's infant mortality rate—the number of babies that die before their first birthday—stands at 8 deaths out of every 1,000 live births. Slightly worse than the rate in Canada, this figure stems in part from the number of poor people who lack health insurance or proper medical care.

State and local governments are in charge of public education. About 75 percent of the nation's elementary and high

A teacher in Mississippi helps a student become familiar with computers, which are a standard learning tool in most schools throughout the country.

schools and 45 percent of the colleges and universities are public institutions. Public education is free through grade 12 and compulsory up to the age of 16 or 17 in most states. Church-run and other private schools are supported by tuition fees charged to students of all ages.

About 97 percent of the people living in the United States can read and write—an average number compared to other developed nations. Most students—about 75 percent—graduate from high school, and more than half of the nation's high-school graduates continue their education at institutions of higher learning.

Language and Literature

Although the U.S. government has never named an official national language, English has been the chief language since the country was founded. Historically, immigrants have used their native tongues in their homes and ethnic neighborhoods, while their children learned English at school.

Some people in cities with large Latino populations believe that their schools and local governments should be able to conduct business in Spanish—the second most common tongue in the United States. But other people argue that the use of a single language helps to unify a nation, and some states have passed laws making English their state's official language.

Writing almost exclusively in English, U.S. authors and poets began forging their own literary style in the mid-1800s. Henry David Thoreau and Oliver Wendell Holmes were among the first to depart from European styles by writing about the United States and its people. Edgar Allan Poe and Nathaniel Hawthorne developed the short story into a respected literary form. Louisa May Alcott wrote novels for young readers. Among the greatest poets of the era were Emily Dickinson, Ralph Waldo Emerson, Henry Wadsworth Longfellow, and Walt Whitman.

F. Scott Fitzgerald chronicled the world of the 1920s—an age of glamour, excess, and moral decline. His novels, such as *The Beautiful and the Damned, Tender is the Night,* and *The Great Gatsby,* did not bring the fame that Fitzgerald craved but gained the author acclaim after his death in 1940.

Author, poet, actress, and teacher, Maya Angelou is most known for her autobiographical works, including *I Know Why the Caged Bird Sings,* which tells the story of a young black girl who grows up during the Great Depression. Worldwide attention was focused on Angelou in 1993, when she read an original work at the inauguration ceremonies of President Bill Clinton.

In the late 1800s, Mark Twain used realistic and comical dialects in portraying his adventurous characters. Edith Wharton described the complexities of New York society at the turn of the century, while Jack London explored the struggle for survival, using the frontiers of the Pacific Northwest as his setting.

Industrialization, World War I, and the Great Depression prompted some writers to look at the social problems facing the country in the early 1900s. Upton Sinclair and John Steinbeck acquainted their readers with the poverty and dangers faced by workers, while novels by Ernest Hemingway and F. Scott Fitzgerald described people in search of adventure and escape. William Faulkner mixed tragedy and comedy in his novels, many of which were set in Mississippi. Willa Cather was one of the first U.S. novelists to create strong female characters.

At the same time—during what became known as the Harlem Renaissance—the black community produced many fine authors. The writings of James Weldon Johnson, Langston Hughes, and Jean Toomer appealed to blacks as well as whites. In the 1930s and 1940s, Richard Wright examined racial discrimination, while Zora Neale Hurston published collections of folklore from the Caribbean and the southern United States.

By the 1950s and 1960s, Jack Kerouac and Allen Ginsberg were breaking new ground with free-flowing prose and poetry. The African American authors Ralph Ellison and James Baldwin probed the experience of growing up black in the United States. The conflicts that arise when Jews abandon their traditions became themes for Saul Bellow and Philip Roth. Southern authors Flannery O'Connor and Katherine Anne Porter wrote novels and short stories that received wide acclaim from readers and critics.

During the second half of the twentieth century, female and Native American

In the 1800s, George Catlin's depictions of Indian life in the western territories fascinated people in the eastern United States. This work shows Plains Indians stalking bison by disguising themselves as other animals. In this way, the hunters could get very close to the bison before firing any arrows.

authors reached a broad audience. Betty Friedan's works helped to launch the women's rights movement of the 1970s. The Sioux writer Vine Deloria, Jr., examined the plight of Native Americans. Popular contemporary authors include Amy Tan, Tom Wolfe, Toni Morrison, Kurt Vonnegut, Jr., and Maya Angelou.

Art, Theater, and Music

Trained by Europeans, many colonial artists made a living painting wealthy families. Talented portraitists of the 1700s include John Singleton Copley and Gilbert Stuart, whose images of George Washington are well known.

By the 1800s and early 1900s, stories of cowboys and Native Americans on the western frontier had captivated the nation. George Catlin toured North America, painting portraits of Indians and their ways of life. Charles Marion Russell won fame for his spirited portrayals of cowboys and cattle.

In New York, the style of abstract expressionism enabled artists to convey their ideas with color instead of with clearly

The painter Georgia O'Keeffe *(pictured in 1926)* used the landscape and materials of the southwestern desert—bare animal bones, wild plants, and rocks—in her works. O'Keeffe lived to be nearly 100 years old, and throughout her long career continued to be inspired by the colors and shapes found near her home in New Mexico.

50

drawn figures. The movement, which started after World War II, brought into the limelight several U.S. artists, including Jackson Pollock and Mark Rothko.

In the early 1960s, Andy Warhol became the leader of the Pop Art movement, which elevated everyday items such as soup cans to the level of artistic symbols. Other famous twentieth-century artists in the United States include Frank Stella, Norman Rockwell, Grandma Moses, and Georgia O'Keeffe.

New York, Chicago, and Los Angeles are the leading centers for professional theater in the United States. Some of the nation's most noteworthy playwrights include Eugene O'Neill, Tennessee Williams, Arthur Miller, Lillian Hellman, Edward Albee, and August Wilson. Musicals—in which the story is told through dialogue, song, and dance—were first used in theater and later in motion pictures. The most famous composers of musical scores include Irving Berlin, George Gershwin, and

Photo by Photofest

Musicals are a hallmark of American theater. Dancers *(above)* perform in a street scene from *West Side Story*, a Broadway musical that later became an award-winning motion picture. The U.S. composer Leonard Bernstein wrote the music for this tale of gang warfare in New York City in the 1950s. Meanwhile, rock and roll—another U.S. musical invention—took the world by storm, when Elvis Presley *(right)* and other singers introduced audiences to new rhythms, dance steps, and instruments.

Courtesy of Hollywood Book & Poster

the teams of Alan Lerner and Frederick Loewe and of Richard Rodgers and Oscar Hammerstein II.

Jazz, the blues, country and western, and rock and roll all originated in the United States. Louis Armstrong, Duke Ellington, and Ella Fitzgerald gained fame as accomplished jazz artists, while Albert King and Billie Holiday sang the blues. Hank Williams stands out among country-and-western singers, and Chuck Berry and Elvis Presley defined early rock and roll. The nation's noteworthy classical composers include Aaron Copland and Leonard Bernstein, both of whom also wrote for the stage.

Sports

Favorite U.S. sports are baseball, football, basketball, and hockey, all of which originated in the nation. Most large cities have at least one professional team. Fans also enjoy watching high-school and college-level competition. Nonprofessional athletes play baseball and softball on sandlot fields throughout the country.

Climate often determines what sporting activities are most popular in a region. Most northern local parks, for example, offer indoor and outdoor hockey arenas that double as ice-skating rinks before and after scheduled games. Hiking and skiing are common pastimes in mountainous areas, while most surfers live near an oceanfront.

Talented young people from throughout the nation train to compete in the Olympics—an international sporting event that is held every two years. U.S. athletes have been successful in both Summer and Winter Games, taking home numerous gold medals in basketball, figure skating, track and field, and swimming.

Courtesy of University of Georgia

Tough young players compete in football games at large and small colleges throughout the country.

Cyclists speed through town during a biking event in Wisconsin.

Texas Rangers' batting sensation Juan Gonzalez swings at a ball during a professional baseball game.

Deep snow and beautiful scenery attract hardy cross-country skiers to northeastern South Dakota.

Ohio is one of the most industrialized U.S. states. Its factories make steel, assemble transportation equipment, produce rubber for tires, and manufacture soap.

4) The Economy

The United States is a leading global economic power and one of the wealthiest nations on earth. The U.S. gross domestic product (GDP)—the value of goods and services produced in the country in a year—is the highest in the world. The nation has benefited from abundant natural resources and highly developed industries.

The U.S. economy is run largely on free enterprise, a system that allows individuals and private companies to establish and control their businesses. Companies own the equipment and materials needed to produce goods, and the operators of the companies determine who to hire and how to make a profit.

The federal government, however, does play a role. Over the years, the government has passed laws to prevent monopolies from forming. It also determines the minimum wage employers can pay to their workers, tries to assure safe working conditions, and sets environmental regulations.

Manufacturing and Trade

Manufacturing accounts for about one-fifth of the country's GDP and employs nearly the same portion of the workforce. Major industrial centers are located in the northeastern and midwestern United States, but a growing number of factories now operate in southern states and along the Pacific coast.

California and Washington specialize in making food products and high-tech goods, such as aircraft, aerospace equipment, computers, and computer software. Older factories in the Great Lakes area furnish much of the nation's iron, steel, and automobiles. Textile mills, food-processing plants, and printing firms dot the northeastern and southeastern United States. Oil refineries and petrochemical businesses are based mainly in mineral-producing states, including Texas and Louisiana.

Of all manufactured goods, transportation equipment—such as cars, trucks, and aircraft—make up the largest sector. Food products, chemicals, machinery, metals, printed materials, petroleum, and coal are other leading moneymakers.

Because of the size of its industrial economy, the United States is the world's most active trading nation. Its primary trading partners are Canada, Japan, Mexico, Britain, and Germany. Major exports are chemicals, motor vehicles and parts, computers, grains, and industrial machinery. Imports include motor vehicles and parts, petroleum, clothing, toys, and metals such as iron and steel. The United States has had a trade deficit since the 1970s, meaning that the country has spent more money to buy foreign goods than it has earned from selling products abroad.

Agriculture

About 98 percent of U.S. territory is considered rural. Yet only 26 percent of the country's population lives in rural areas, and just 9 percent of the workforce is employed in farming.

Although the United States creates only 2 percent of its GDP from farming, the nation leads the world in agricultural output. Farms and ranches in the United States supply about half of the world's corn, 20 percent of its meat, and just

A farmer on the Great Plains of South Dakota harvests his wheat crop. Nationwide, farmers grow roughly 10 percent of the world's wheat.

over 10 percent of its wheat. The United States produces enough to feed the nation's population and exports about 30 percent of the country's harvest globally.

Expansive tracts of fertile land, up-to-date machinery, and modern methods of cultivation help account for the nation's farming productivity. But the high costs of keeping up with current technology—as well as some modern farming methods—are changing agriculture. Since the early 1900s, the number of small, family-owned farms in the United States has steadily decreased. Meanwhile, the number of large, corporate-run farms has increased. These large-scale farms usually can afford the most advanced equipment and do not require a huge workforce. As a result, the number of agricultural workers is falling as production increases.

The country's leading farm products are beef, milk, corn, soybeans, poultry, eggs, hogs, wheat, and cotton. Also high on the list are hay, tobacco, citrus fruits, potatoes, and peanuts. Ranchers and farmers in the Great Plains raise most of the na-

Blooming potato plants blanket a field in northern Maine, which is the nation's third largest potato producer after Idaho and Washington State.

Independent Picture Service

Piled high with coal dug from Wyoming's mines, a train brings the fuel to power stations throughout the country.

Photo © Scott T. Smith

A row of modern windmills helps harness the force of wind as a non-polluting energy source. As energy demands in the United States rise, developers try to find new ways to produce electrical power.

tion's beef cattle, wheat, and corn. Dairy cattle, grains, and potatoes are grown on farms throughout the Central Lowlands. Tobacco and peanuts thrive in the warm climate of the southern states. Vegetables and citrus fruits are key exports of Florida, California, and Hawaii.

Mining and Energy

Mining contributes 1 percent to the nation's GDP and employs 1 percent of the workforce. The sale of petroleum, natural gas, and coal brings in the most money. Other important minerals include copper, gold, granite, iron ore, limestone, phosphate rock, and salt.

Privately owned mining companies drill for oil in Alaska, Texas, California, and from onshore and offshore wells along the Gulf of Mexico. Miners extract much of the nation's coal in the Appalachians and Wyoming. Nevada yields the most gold.

The United States is the world's second largest producer of petroleum, but the country remains the single greatest consumer of this limited resource. As a result, the United States must import about 30 percent of the oil it needs to run industries and automobiles.

A limited global oil supply has led researchers to explore alternative fuel sources, such as solar energy and wind power. Scientists have also developed methods to convert other energy-producing resources—including coal, oil shale, and bituminous sands—into synthetic oils.

Vehicles, factories, and homes consume a vast amount of energy in the United States. Petroleum meets about 40 percent of the demand, while coal and natural gas each contribute about 25 percent. Nuclear and hydroelectric power plants account for the remaining 10 percent. Public opposition and the high cost of construction have stopped the building of additional nuclear power facilities in the United States.

Major hydroelectric projects in the United States include the Hoover Dam along the Arizona-Nevada border. The huge structure diverts the Colorado River to supply energy and water to Arizona, Nevada, and California. The Grand Coulee Dam, on the Columbia River in Washington State, is the greatest single source of waterpower in the United States.

Photo by Robert Boyer/New England Stock Photo

Photo by Craig Blouin

Forestry and Fishing

The United States is one of the world's leading producers of timber. Woodlands cover about one-third of the country, with the largest tracts located in Alaska and in the western United States. The U.S. government has set aside about two-thirds of the nation's forested land for commercial use. Forest products include lumber, pulp, turpentine, wood tar, and rosin (a natural substance used to make varnish and other goods).

Logs felled in Alabama *(above)* await further processing. A mill in New Hampshire *(left)* manufactures writing paper, paper bags, and paper towels from the state's forests.

Since colonial times, farmers and developers have cleared forests to create farmland and urban areas. To guarantee a steady supply of timber, foresters now manage government-owned timberlands. Workers use different methods of harvesting and replanting to get the maximum amount of timber, while maintaining a healthy forest for future supplies.

Commercial fishers in the United States harvest about six million tons of fish and shellfish annually. The largest catches come from the Gulf of Mexico, which supplies mainly oysters, shrimps, and menhaden. Crews in the Pacific Ocean net a variety of fish and shellfish, including cod, crab, salmon, and tuna. Boats along the Atlantic coast haul in cod, flounder, clams, lobsters, and oysters.

Water pollution and overfishing have damaged some of the nation's fishing grounds. To help ensure that stocks of fish can survive, the United States sets strict quotas for certain species and severely limits the number of fishing vessels that can operate in overfished areas.

Photo by Middleton Evans

Fishing crews in Maryland's section of the Chesapeake Bay use linked baskets to haul in oysters. Pollution has decreased the bay's catch, and Maryland and nearby states are cooperating to clean up the waterway.

Transportation and Tourism

People in the United States rely heavily on privately owned automobiles for personal transportation, using nearly four million miles of roads. Crisscrossing the nation is a vast network of interstate highways that links major cities. The interstate system offers commercial trucks a straightforward means of delivering the country's goods.

Most U.S. railroad companies earn the bulk of their income from hauling cargo.

But many people, especially in the northeastern United States, rely on commuter trains to get to and from work. Travel by passenger train began to disappear in the 1950s and 1960s, as other forms of transportation, such as buses and automobiles, became commonplace. To help save this industry, the U.S. government established a railroad company called Amtrak in the 1970s to handle intercity rail traffic.

In the nation's largest metropolitan areas, trains and subways carry commu-

Photo © Ed Kashi

Highways crisscross the United States, making it possible for motorists not only to commute to work but also to travel at high speeds from coast to coast.

The Union Pacific Railroad *(right)*—which laid half the track to give the United States its first coast-to-coast rail link in the 1860s—still operates in the Great Plains. A barge *(below)* makes its way down the Mississippi River to the huge port of New Orleans, Louisiana, which handles much of the cargo shipped from the United States.

ters in and out of town. But the most widely used form of urban public transportation is the bus. Several U.S. cities—including Fort Worth in Texas and San Diego and San Jose in California—have built light-rail transit systems, which are less expensive than most conventional means of transportation.

About 50 ports—situated on U.S. waterways and coasts—handle 15 percent of the nation's freight. The ports at New Orleans, New York, Houston, and Los Angeles see the most traffic. Many freighters and ships on the Mississippi River system enter the Great Lakes by way of the port of Chicago on Lake Michigan. Commercial airlines also carry freight, but most of their customers are passengers.

Airports, which are located near every sizable U.S. city, welcome flights from throughout the country. Regional hubs provide local services, and most of the larger airports handle international traffic. Chicago's O'Hare is the world's busiest airport.

Music lovers flock to the coastal city of Newport, Rhode Island, to attend the state's annual jazz festival.

Nearly 40 million tourists from all over the world visit the United States every year. These vacationers pump $40 billion into the U.S. economy. The largest number of visitors comes from Canada, Mexico, and Japan.

World-famous museums, cultural performances, and landmarks draw about 17 million people every year to New York—one of the world's most visited cities. The beaches and warm weather of Florida, California, and Hawaii have made these states major U.S. tourism centers for anglers, scuba divers, and sunbathers. In California and Florida, amusement parks entertain millions every year.

Carved into the Black Hills of South Dakota, Mount Rushmore National Memorial features the faces (from left to right) of U.S. presidents George Washington, Thomas Jefferson, Theodore Roosevelt, and Abraham Lincoln.

At Walt Disney World—a resort in Orlando, Florida—the Magic Kingdom brings to life animal characters made famous through the Disney studio's cartoons and animated films.

The rugged terrain of Oregon, Washington, Montana, Idaho, and Colorado challenges mountain climbers and hikers. Resorts in the Rocky Mountains and in the Sierra Nevada attract skiers of all skill levels. At national parks such as Yellowstone, Yosemite, Grand Teton, and Grand Canyon, campers enjoy scenic wildernesses, some of which have been protected by federal law for more than a century.

The Future

Blessed with a wealth of natural resources, a relatively strong economy, and an innovative population, the United States is among the most advanced and stable nations in the world. This standing has enabled the country's citizens to achieve a high standard of living. The United States has also become a major force in the global marketplace, using international trade agreements to help U.S. corporations compete successfully worldwide.

In a world that continues to link economic weight with political power, the United States is often accused by other nations of abusing its global influence. Some citizens believe that U.S. leaders should spend the country's money on domestic programs to ensure internal stability and to promote higher standards of living. Other citizens argue that global responsibility goes hand in hand with global economic clout. As the world's sole superpower, the United States will be striving to juggle these two conflicting points of view as it heads toward the twenty-first century.

Vacationers enjoy the scenery along a guided trail in Canyonlands National Park, Utah.

Index